Praise for Roseann Lloyd

"The poems in Roseann Lloy'd new poetry collection take us on a sister's unflinching exploration into her grief, her family's grief, for a brother lost in the wilderness. She brings us with her into the deep waters of being a sister. She eloquently expresses the past shared with her brother. His absence breathes upon the present and evokes other disappearances—children missing in Iraq, Jacob Wetterling abducted, climbers lost on Everest, a college student drowned. These are visceral poems, full of verbal energy and rich patterns of sound—Lloyd's lines are allowed to breathe and they move about in always interesting forms. The powerful prose poem, "Messing Around in Boats," shows us her mother reading *Wind in the Willows: 'Look, look, cries my brother, he's heading for the road, he's heading for the river, he's getting away!'* I have never been so moved by a book of poetry."

—Mary Kay Rummel, author of *What's Left is the Singing*

"*The Boy Who Slept Under the Stars* is Roseann Lloyd's magnificent tribute to her brother and to her love for him. In this book, she movingly portrays the intimacy of family—in suffering as well as in affection and fun. These poems have much to say that is not only moving, but healing. As the poems weave together experiences from many times, and other families and places, they broaden the reader's sensitivity to life's inevitable struggles. Shining through it all is a deep compassion for all loss and heartbreak on this earth."

—Nancy Paddock, author of *A Song at Twilight: Of Alzheimer's and Love*

" 'You settle your bones into a river of words,' and go with Roseann Lloyd's meander through years of brother memories. I think of these pieces as 'walking poems,' and their reading is an enactment of some new, welcome, moving ritual of grief and loss."

—Nor Hall, author of *The Moon and the Virgin: Reflections on the Archetypal Feminine*

BOOKS BY ROSEANN LLOYD:

POETRY

Because of the Light, (Holy Cow! Press, 2003)

War Baby Express, (Holy Cow! Press, 1996)

Tap Dancing for Big Mom, (New Rivers Press, 1986)

ANTHOLOGY, EDITOR

Looking for Home: Women Writing About Exile,

with Deborah Keenan, (Milkweed Editions, 1990)

NONFICTION

True Selves: Twelve-Step Recovery from Codependency,

with Merle Fossum, (Hazelden/Harper, 1991)

JourneyNotes: Writing for Recovery and Spiritual Growth,

with Richard Solly, (Hazelden/Harper, 1989, Ballentine Edition, 1992)

TRANSLATION

The House with the Blind Glass Windows (co-translated),

a contemporary Norwegian novel by Herbjørg Wassmo, (Seal Press, 1995)

THE BOY WHO SLEPT UNDER THE STARS

A Memoir in Poetry

Roseann Lloyd

Holy Cow! Press :: Duluth, Minnesota :: 2012

Roseann Lloyd is a fiscal year 2011 recipient of an Artist Initiative grant from the Minnesota State Arts Board. This activity is made possible in part by a grant from the Minnesota State Arts Board, through an appropriation by the Minnesota State Legislature and by a a grant from the National Endowment for the Arts.

The author would like to acknowledge the editors and staff of the following journals (print and online) for publishing the following poems:

"April, Baby," "The Family of Frederico García Lorca Stands against the Exhumation of His Remains," "Heartland MIA," *Pemmican*, Summer, 2010; "Cold up North," *Dust & Fire: Writing & Art by Women 2011*; "The Labyrinth, Winter Solstice," *Askew*: Issue #5 Fall/Winter 2008; "What It Was Like Today: November 13, 2005," *Tattoo Highway 19* Summer/Fall 2009; "First Summers and the Last: The Boy Who Slept Under the Stars," forthcoming in *Askew*. Thanks to Jim Rogers for the New and Nearby Reading Series at Trotter's Cafe, St. Paul, Minnesota, and for publishing community chapbooks to raise money for food shelves; "The Labyrinth in Winter" appears in *The Sun Shines, the Day is On: Poems of Gratitude*, 2010; "In My Poems Since You Left Us" appears in *The Inside of a Butternut Squash*, 2011.

Library of Congress Cataloging-in-Publication Data
Lloyd, Roseann.
The boy who slept under the stars : a memoir in poetry / Roseann Lloyd.
p. cm.
ISBN 978-0-9833254-8-2 (alk. Paper)
1. Brothers—Poetry. 2. Missing persons—Poetry. 3. Boundary Waters Canoe Area (Minn.)—Poetry. I. Title.
PS3562.L76B69 2012
811'.54 — dc23 2012009674

This project is supported in part by gifts from generous individual donors. Holy Cow! Press books are distributed to the trade by: Consortium Book Sales & Distribution, c/o Perseus Distribution, 210 American Drive, Jackson, TN 38301.

For personal inquiries, write to: Holy Cow! Press, Post Office Box 3170, Mount Royal Station, Duluth, Minnesota 55803.

Please visit our website: www.holycowpress.org

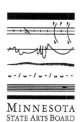

MINNESOTA
STATE ARTS BOARD

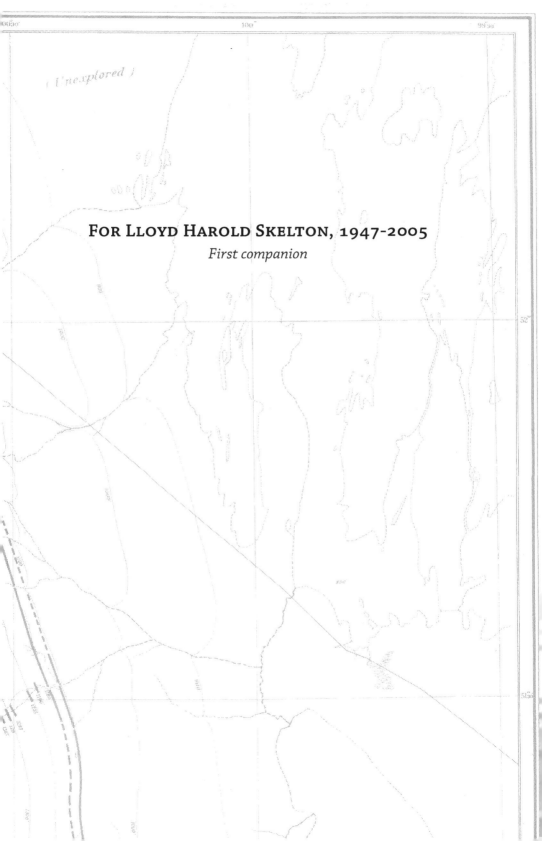

FOR LLOYD HAROLD SKELTON, 1947-2005

First companion

CONTENTS

Part One: Circumambulation: Without a Body to Mourn

Walker, there is no path.
You make your path as you walk.
—Antonio Machado

Without a body to mourn
cognition is blocked by unfamiliarity.
—Pauline Boss

Neither Here Nor There:
What They Said

It's been two weeks since my brother Lloyd said he'd be back, I said to my friend. We breathed the moist air of linden tree, silver maples. Still June, the humidity hadn't hit us yet. *He promised me. He said he'd help me out after my foot surgery.* She quoted a poem, *He's not lost, the trees in the forest know where he is.* That day a deputy had found his van on a back road in the Boundary Waters, far from where he said he was going. His friends rushed to help Search and Rescue, to walk the cold trail, to watch the orange rubber boats drop into the clear water, to witness his clothes spread along the untended trail to Whisky Jack Lake. One friend said, *He was wired for the wilderness.* A woman in Ely said, *He was a legend up here—he went places I wouldn't go.*

By July, the hope of rescue had gone. *I'm sorry we couldn't bring Lloyd home,* his friend Laura said at the memorial service. July 1st. I still saw his body lying in the woods, slowly sinking into the boggy June earth. Maybe he wouldn't have minded his bones resting there. Grade school friends teased us for our last name: *Hey, Skelton ... The toe bone's connected to the heel bone, the heel bone's connected to the foot bone ...* He died in a place he loved. How many people can say that? Woods by the water. Trillium, Lady's Slipper, Dutchman's Britches. *His* Boundary Waters, *his* land and water, *his* edge of heaven.

His disappearance was a personal offense to all those who love that endless maze and claim it for their own. A friend told me later, *When I heard about your brother, I took my dog and went up north to camp, to paint more water and stars.* Other people asked, *How could this happen?* As if the Boundary Waters is paradise— surely they haven't ever paddled a big lake like Saganaga in a storm, waves tipping the canoe, rain erasing the four directions like watercolors.

Sinking into stormy memory, I took on another consolation: Lloyd's hatred of embalming. He'd recoiled when we saw our younger brother's body laid out, his swollen neck unable to be doctored by the undertaker. Oh, Philip. *No embalming, no embalming,* Lloyd said when our father died some thirty years later. But that story is neither here nor there. This is the story of the way I made it through that first summer, and the next five summers, learning to walk again, wiped out by sorrow. *He died in a place he loved. When will a hiker stumble on his body?*

Sometime along summer's beautiful turning, the sheriff told us there wouldn't be another search. *By this length of time after a death,* he said, slowly, gently—awkwardly, even—*we won't be able to find a body. By now the animals will have taken him.* Silence followed the sheriff's sentence. When I reported it to friends, they said, *What? The animals?* My daughter said, *I thought bears ate blueberries.* Our mother said, *What kind of animal could haul off a grown man?* My husband said, *Everybody is protein for somebody.* Nightmares conjured up mountain lions, bobcats, cougars. The sheriff added, *The most we can hope for—someday a hiker will come across his skull.* His skull? The skull would tell us nothing about his suffering. It wouldn't tell us if his feet gave out, or his lungs, or his heart. It wouldn't even tell us the location of his death.

The skull only leads us back to mysteries, to childhood, to playing in the dark, to singing ... *the head bone's connected to the neck bone*. The skull leads us to harvest and Halloween, dressing our kids up in scary costumes, that one twilight when my brother and I draped vines and stalks from the compost heap on our heads and ran towards the kids singing out, *We're the ghosts of the compost*. The skull has a candle in it; it leads us back in time to Shakespeare; forward to latter day saints of mystery, Abby, the TV forensic scientist with her skull T-shirt. *Hey, Bones, what's shakin'?*

COLD UP NORTH

my skull a terrarium of regrets
—Spencer Reece

It was in that little cabin Up North
in that first cold summer of sorrow
where I sat in the cushioned rocker
and wrapped that heavy shawl around me
like a tiny woman by a winter hearth,
an electric heater the size of a bread box
at my feet, that a wail finally came up
from my gut listening/not listening/
to *Highway 61 Revisited* over and
over until the wailing slowed to tears
and rocking, slowed to a vision of my
brother climbing up our roof to find
the chink in the chimney that the bats
crawled in and me yelling at him,
Get down before you break your neck
and then the memory of arguing over
who owned which Dylan records,
the ones that now gather mice
in someone else's basement.
                              No longer cold,
I stood up. Took a photo of the writing desk
where I had written no words all day.
Red journal, coffee cup, plate of pears.

Then I took a photo of a painting on the wall,
a lupine meadow, it was—fuchsias, pinks, indigo—
and then I took a photo of the woodcut of
two crows and *Why?* I wondered
when I could've stepped outside
for photos of real lupine and real crows
or I could've left the camera behind
and picked up lupine pods and a crow feather.
Maybe even found a whole silky wing. But no.
I turned back to the chair with its deep well
where nobody was sitting now, the shawl
still resting on the arms. Yes.
I took a picture of that empty chair.

MY BROTHER'S TEARS

1

Once I heard howling and ran down the dirt road,
a clot of children bending over blood spraying—
Lloyd's fourth finger clamped and
sliced between the metal cock
and wooden barrel of his BB gun. His arm
trying to shake it loose.

The other little kids didn't have the strength
to uncock it, jammed as it was into the
finger's raw flesh, muscle and blood.

I grabbed that wooden stock
with one hand, the metal with the other.
Steady, I jerked it, alligator's jaw, open.
Freed his bloody finger. Walked him
to the house, arm around his shoulder.
Didn't say *Stop wailing, honey.*

2

After that day, he didn't cry.
Not during our father's brow beatings.
Not after the slaps, the spankings,
and worse. No wails, no howling.

There were no more tears. Tears,
I knew, would mean *Daddy won.*

No tears years later when our brother Philip died,
his frozen face, a dam on pain.

3
I went to our father's funeral because Lloyd
asked me to. We sat in small pews
in the small chapel of the Jefferson Barracks,
St. Louis home of soldiers since the Civil War.

My brother's shoulders started shaking.
I put my arm around his bony wings,
felt his scarce body through the thin
navy blue wool. Left my arm there lightly.
As long as he sobbed.

Gun shots stopped our tears cold.
The military salute startled us,
as if our father had risen one more time
to bellow, *This belt will turn you into
a Christian gentleman.*

4
Once at the French Meadow restaurant
Lloyd and I lunched in spring sun.
He told me a story about a kayaking
trip to Indonesia, where his friend met
two girls who'd lost their parents in a storm.
Tsunami swallowed their fishing boat, too.

Now the girls, not yet teenagers,
fish by themselves for food.
Their boat, a slab of Styrofoam.

Styrofoam. My brother stuttered
over the word, hulked and sobbed,
right there in the restaurant, all the pain
of the world, our baguette on the table
taken for granted. His tears made
his blue eyes bigger, made him look more
like the boy shaking a BB gun in agony
than a man easing a kayak through
canyons of white water rapids.

5
So much can be said for the child
Lloyd once was—the boy
he carries in his heart.

First Summers and the Last:
The Boy Who Slept Under the Stars

the summer our mother held Lloyd in a rocking chair
a small flannel comma, the first memory of my life

chubby summer—my longed-for companion
kept slipping off my lap

the no-talking summer
my job to say *He's bashful, what do you want?*

and then his first sentence summer
Maybe Y-S, maybe N-O
(who knew it would be his life-time strategy?)

puppy summer all over the bushes and yard:
I got him in trouble yelling
Mama, Lloyd's kissing Brownie on the mouth

me-making-roads-in-the-gravel-driveway summer
his John Deere trucks zooming across boulders
the *dump twuck* loaded to overflowing

our own private radio summer:
Velveeta, lettuce, and mayonnaise sandwiches in our little room
Sunday nights in the attic: *The Lone Ranger,*
Sergeant Preston of the Canadian Mounties

running in the dark summer:
Ghost and *Kick the Can*
crawling under the bushes on our elbows like soldiers at war
getting as far as the cornfield: hiding

lying on the grass summer, dozing
looking at the stars

2
his last summer, the summer he got out his yellow kayak
said he wanted to get on with it, if only the rain would stop

the summer our sister took me shopping for clothes
so I'd look pretty in my wheelchair after surgery
and he said, *You always look pretty to me*

the summer he wheeled me to the Birchwood Café
threatening revenge for telling him ghost stories—
those lions in the basement

genealogy summer: *which cousin went to rehab*
before the Branson Reunion?

the summer he confessed that the childhood word
I'd invented to tease him (still secret)
has been his computer password all this time

the summer he didn't want to leave his cat, dying of cancer

the summer we talked about mysteries

the lying on the grass summer,
looking at the stars

Memory: Layers like Mica

I thought for a long time that the first memory of my life, not counting the sounds of the cicadas, or locusts as we called them, was my new baby brother Lloyd on our mother's lap in my gramma's bedroom, the room dim, and he only a soft shape that quickly changed to a shape much chubbier than my biggest doll, but when our dad went into a nursing home in St. Louis, decades later, Lloyd, now a strong and lanky man, hauled the three lion chairs that had been in Gramma Emily's house to Minnesota. Then I saw a toddler—that would be me—walking up to one of those lions and my angle of vision shifted from the bird's eye view to the floor where I was walking. I looked up and saw the ferocious head and open jaw of this beast. I lifted my finger up towards the teeth and pointed and paused and finally put my finger in the mouth to see if the teeth would chomp down and eat it. No matter how many times I tried this, every visit to Gramma Emily's, I was always safe and I was way too short to have a baby brother yet, so this memory must have come first when I was on my own navigating the wilds of the houses of our kin. Later, when my brother did come along he liked to rub down the horse hair seat—we did that together— and then we would rub it the wrong way and jump at the prick- les. He loved anything to do with horses, cows, and cowboys. All this makes me think that maybe testing the lion's mouth truly is my first memory and my brother liked knowing I had gone first and made the way clear for him and that's why he insisted I take one of the chairs so many years later. I was scared it would bring our dad's energy into our home until my therapist said, *Think of it as your gramma's, she would want you to have it* and that did the trick. *It was the only nice furniture she ever had.* The chair brings layers of memory shifting like mica turning its layers in light: All the scary stories I told the little kids, my brother actually looking into the camera in his cowboy suit, the mountain lions in my nightmares when he went missing, the postcard I bought in the British Museum, for no reason, I thought, of a lion mauling a man. When I tell my brother's daughter how I was once so little I had to reach up to test the teeth, she says *You've told me that already,* so I'm thinking next time I'll tell her about her dad, my brother, patting the horsehair. How he loved cowboys. How he wrote at school, *Grandpa love him cowes.* How he smiled at me, *You have to have one of the chairs.* How he felt safe surrounded by the smell of horse and straw.

Lloyd Lloyd

When I got divorced the first time I wanted to change my name to something new not go back to my dad's name **Skelton**, and not be **Rosie Bones** again, so I looked back in the family tree and the name with most good feeling was **Lloyd** for my grandpa who held me on his lap in his seersucker suit and Gramma who listened to my stories and read me poems. Even though we thought the name was Welsh we didn't have any real proof because those Lloyd family stories got lost somehow during the War Between the States. Uncle Jack Lloyd said *his* grandpa William Loyd didn't talk about the past because he was a bootlegger which is really an aggravating excuse. Why would that stop anyone from saying he was Welsh?

When I came into the possession of that William H. Loyd's (yes, spelled with one **L**) discharge paper from the Union Army in Mississippi, I asked second cousin Christina if she knew where the **Lloyds** came from (even though she's not a Lloyd) and she said her mother Verna Lee said that they came from Carroll County, Arkansas, and when the War started the family split apart, that brother-against-brother thing. But in this case, it was the father who stood with the Rebs and son who joined up with the Yankees. That's how the family stories got lost. War and anger and sorrow cut off a branch of the family tree.

William H. Loyd crossed the Mason-Dixon line, settled in Salem, Missouri, bootleg country, now meth country, which you can see in the movie **Winter's Bone**, but he bankrolled his children into town and they all (both boys and girls) went into legit business and by the time I came along **Lloyd** was an okay name in terms of The Law. They sent their children to college, especially the girls; the women finished their degrees.

All my other family names had one thing or another working against them as a surname: the **Andersons** from Scotland had a bland sound, trailing depressive genes; the Irish **Hoseys** from Pennsylvania would've made my name **Rosie Posey Hosey**. Don't get me wrong, Hosey is a fine name for a man who fought for **Meads 5th** in the battle for Chattanooga but not for me (*ashes ashes all fall down*). I considered, too, the names on my dad's side, the ones who worked their way from Virginia to the Appalachians then the Ozarks. **Stubblefield** a testimony to the struggle to raise crops in rocky hills. **Meador**, that romantic link to *meadow*, my pen name in grade school. Some said my grandmother Emily's mother, Lucy Ann **Boothe** was a cousin of John Wilkes Booth, in spite of the addition of *e*. Boothe was not a lineage I wanted to follow, not to mention the relative who drove a wagonload of enslaved people to Waco, Texas, leaving his white wife to defend their homestead against Yankee invaders.

In the end, then, I forsook **Rosie Bones** for **Lloyd**. It brought its own problems. It does mean *gray* in Welsh and so suggests the gray gloomy nature of the British Isles and the family tree. But it sounds more interesting than the ordinary name **Anderson**, Son of Anders, my link to Scandinavia. And you can't beat those genes: *Mornings were reserved for remorse and sweet tea* ... For years after the name change, we called my brother *Lloyd Lloyd* too. Of course, he never made it legal. But at family gatherings it was real. I couldn't say it without putting my arm around him and laughing.

Lloyd Lloyd, why aren't you here to talk over all these old family stories with me?

MESSING AROUND IN BOATS

In or out of'em, it doesn't matter. Nothing seems really to matter,
that's the charm of it. Whether you get away, or whether you
don't; whether you arrive at your destination or whether you reach
somewhere else, or whether you never get anywhere at all...
—Kenneth Grahame, *Wind in the Willows*

Sometimes our mother read to us on the couch before bed, even though we were so many different ages. What I liked about the couch was leaning against Lloyd with my arm behind him, leaning into our mother to see the pictures closest up after the little kids started playing on the rug. My brother would beg for *Wind in the Willows*—the ins and outs of river life, Mole, Ratty, Badger, and Mr. Toad, all *simply messing around in boats*. I imagined being Mole and having a cozy home under the roots by the water; my brother liked to *see* all the boats—punts, houseboats, the riverboat drawn by a horse and so forth—going every which way. He was waiting for the Mad Mr. Toad to leap into a vehicle of any sort and when he did, like when he got on the riverboat disguised as a washer woman, my brother exhaled with a half cry of glee. Since he didn't talk much, his cry of glee was all the more impressive. Another picture showed a red and brown caravan tipping precariously half way into the ditch, into which it did indeed fall, the horse somehow flying free. We were worried Mr. Toad might get hurt in that tumble.

After all these years the fears and worries and colors come back in an instant. The picture that leaps to my mind most often is the picture of Mad Mr. Toad slowly knotting sheets together in the bedroom of his castle, Toad Hall, where his friends have imprisoned him to keep him out of trouble—so many injuries and speeding tickets. At last he has a long rope of sheets all tied together. He is clever, Mr. Toad. He knots one end to the leg of a bedstead and flings the other end out the tall stone window. Then he must crab his way up the sheet to the window and out! rappelling down oh so many gigantic stories to the ground! *Look, look,* cries my brother, *he's heading for the road, he's heading for the river, he's getting away!*

But Were You Mad?

Hell, yes, I was mad. Mad that he left in the afternoon for a day hike without taking into account his tremor, his cigarettes. Mad at his belief that his luck and stamina would go on forever. Yes, I was mad. Mad that he told his buddy at the outfitters that he'd head to the North Shore but didn't. Didn't tell anyone he was heading for the Echo Trail. Mad that he promised me *Tuesday*. Mad that others said, *He always does this and then turns up*. Mad at myself. I didn't report him missing. Mad that I spent days calling every hospital in Northern Minnesota to see if they had a patient with amnesia, falling in love with a nurse like in the old black and white movies. Mad that we didn't know where he was—where Search and Rescue should begin the search. Mad that the Forest Service doesn't track the day hike entry permits at trailheads—volunteers collect those paper slips for a count of how many hikers use the trail. Mad that the portage trails are kept up better than the hiking trails.

Mad that deputies drove all those roads for days until one came upon my brother's van, tucked away behind trees in the parking lot, **Entry Point #20** off the Echo Trail. Mad that when the Virginia, Minnesota police put crime scene tape around his trail of clothes, some canoeists hesitated, *Is a serial killer on the loose in the Boundary Waters?* Mad that people picked up his clothing, that is, *evidence*. But evidence of what? Mad that

he brought me a stack of books that triggered my allergies—
they'd sucked up his second-hand smoke like a girl holding
her breath out of spite. Mad that I sent them to Goodwill.
Mad I didn't write down all the titles of his favorite books.
Mad at his tremor. Mad he didn't come back. Yes, that's it. I
was mad.

AUTUMNAL

For some reason, the worst is when I'm in the car by myself.
—Corine McCandless, whose brother died in Alaska

For me it was those *Spanish: Learn in Your Car CDs.*
I'd be practicing verb conjugations and a phrase

or a sentence would leap out, and it was all over
for the day: *El bosque está oscuro.*

The forest is dark. *Repite por favor.*
El bosque está oscuro. The forest is dark.

And then there was Halloween. Driving home
from the Birchwood in late afternoon, I saw a man

lying face down in yellow maple leaves, a red checkered shirt,
old khaki pants, shoes stuffed with straw.

Who moved my brother to this ordinary yard
so far from the North Woods?

What It Was Like Today: November 13, 2005

Usually when I wake up, Jim's left the bed, already in our study working. Today I burrow into his chest, sleep with my head on his heart for another hour.

*

Last Tuesday night I turned the car left too soon. I mistook the sidewalk for the driveway. *Not to worry,* the doctor said. *It's not glaucoma, not mood disorder, just heavy lids.*

*

A November Sunday morning, the first gray day, still warm: Jim brings espresso with chocolate and chili pepper biscotti. Lovely south window brings clouds.

*

Heavy lids: sleepiness, Peter Lorre, all the noir movies, cigarettes, lizards, Marlene Dietrich, cartoons of lizards, fedoras, the Raymond Chandler collection my brother gave me the day before he left, last June.

*

We don't talk in the morning until Jim comes with the tray, opens the shades. Today he tells me the Italian story of Pinocchio, noting the parts Disney left out: the constant presence of the woman with hair blue as a blackbird's.

*

Elegant: the word my brother's friends use to describe him, climbing a cliff face.

*

Today over espresso, I ask Jim if he's in the mood for roast chicken for dinner. Sweet potatoes or squash? We'll practice Thanksgiving without my brother, who always started doing the dishes without saying a word.

*

Instead of surgery, I could get a *vertical eyebrow piercing* at St. Sabrina's Parlor in Purgatory but the skin would drape like a velvet theater curtain over my eye.

*

My brother's not in the Hudson Bay, not in Yosemite, not at T.G.I.Friday's, not at home not answering my calls. Sometimes, I sense him behind my left shoulder, murmuring, *I know I let you down. I'm here for you now.*

*

Later today, when I'm up on the roof deck practicing my Greek dance, leading with the left, I will leave no shadow. *Gray November, you have arrived late this year, but I remember you, oh yes, I remember.*

*

Ok, so I've ranted and raved for years against cosmetic surgery, and this is the very thing I need? Say it: *an eye tuck.*

*

Last week, one of my students read out loud her childhood memoir about catching roly-poly bugs. *Of the shrimp family, curling in moist dirt and grass*. I saw my brother's small hands, fiddling, in the early summer grass.

*

I call Christine, tell her about the heavy eyelids, ask if she can teach my class when I have surgery. She sighs, *Dear heart, you've seen too much of the world*.

*

Jim cringes when I joke about *piercings*. He loves light pajamas, styled like *The Thin Man's*, even in winter.

*

Last spring, at a family party, my brother joked, *What if one of us writes an autobiography someday?* Startled, I wanted to shake him, state the obvious—*but I've already written my autobiography. In the poems: layered and coppery agates.*

*

Reading saves me. Fat fiction into the night. A bright light on my left side, for my noir eyes, for the November dark that already blankets us at 4:30.

*

I was angry—no, out of my mind—when my brother's daughter had to clean out his van. Had to pour out the vodka he left, by the half gallon. We must not torment ourselves with happy endings we can't make happen.

*

I pretend that the reason my left eye droops worse than my right is that it's closer to my heart.

*

Our grief-stricken mother finds comfort in her doctor's story of hypothermia: *He probably closed his eyes and curled up in a fetal position under a tree. He felt no pain. No pain at all.*

*

Jim walks around the house, practicing his Italian. I don't understand a word he says but I always answer: *I love it when you speak Italian, baby.*

*

Sunday naptime, I embody the roly-poly bug: round, safe, silent, blind.

*

Now that my eyelids cast all my life in shadow, the shadows live alongside my tender pleasures, in the center: *Jim's chest. Cardinals on the balcony. Norwegian goat cheese on toast.* Anger, guilt, betrayal, sadness—they show up there. That is, *here.*

*

I'm here for you, my brother reassures me. *It's ok,* I say, *I know, I know.* I notice I'm repeating myself.

*

The gray cloak of sisterhood slips from my shoulders: Tell me, what shape will my heart take, next shift?

*

Jim's long legs tangle the bed clothes every night. Before we lie down to sleep again, he carefully tucks in my side of the bed.

*

My brother's missing body, somewhere in the North Woods, makes Whitman literal: *I bequeath myself to the dirt to grow from the grass I love / If you want me again look for me under your boot-soles.*

*

After my surgeries, sometime in the spring, I'll walk clear-eyed along the river. Light-footed in my heavy shoes. As in my former. Life. Here.

My Assigned Humans and Myself

will gather for the assigned holiday
but we'll keep it low-key   a bare bones
menu   one kind of potatoes
white   mashed   with the turkey—
store-bought pies with ice cream
if your daughter forgets to bring
the peas   we'll enjoy our

                                bare bones
menu in this country of assigned
abundance   mahi mahi kiwi ginger
all imported   we'll think of childhood
mottos   *the clean plate club*
for our missing one

                          the one the yellow
mums on the table honor   the one
who got an assignment   Up North
last summer   sure the centerpiece is
pretty but also a warning he won't
be washing dishes

                      when we're done
as usual on assigned holidays
somebody will get worked up
go out to the parking lot to smoke
what of it?   Gilda Radner used to say:
it's always something and if the

bare bones menu causes
too much anxiety?
                    we can always fall
back on turkey pot pies   really   it's
okay so do a quick run-through of
your assignment: olives and celery
Relish it!   and throw in *Home Alone*
your loved one's schema for outwitting
The Mind Police   even if nobody
will watch it
                    for fear laughing
might make us cry

MIRROR: SOLSTICE SUN

1   Physical Therapy

Suzanne lifts my arms in the air
turns me to face the mirror. *Look,*
she says, *you have a dancer's body.*

If I squint, I see a dancer,
but she's a stranger, a gypsy,
not the me who trips and falls.

Suzanne lectures me, *You must*
strengthen your core to support your legs
which hold your ankles. Steady.

Look, she says again, *lift*
your arms up and down as though
they're wings.

You don't need weights to
exercise your arms—they're so long,
their weight alone is enough.

Do you see? You're a bird taking off—
heron, raven, swan. Remember. Once
upon a time we all had wings.

2   Better Late

I give Suzanne and her exuberance a nod,
but when she leads me to the puffy half moon
of a balance mat, I wobble, tip, catch
myself from falling. Pictures of *dancer*
and *heron* give way to *newborn pony* and *giraffe*.

My tipping triggers voices: hoots
and cat calls: *Look out, klutz. Space*
cadet. Hey, Poet, head in the clouds,
watch where you're going.

Never mind all that.
My surgeon set things straight:
Said, *Your problem is structural,*
not psychological. Your arches rise
too high from the ground. He banished
that *klutz* forever. Repaired those tendons
shredded like string cheese.

Now I say *better late than never*
with true passion, without shame
for the time I fell on that Norwegian boy
who was teaching me the mazurka,
and the time I popped an ankle tendon
climbing cliffs at Taylor's Falls.

Yes, *better late.* I trip up the stairs
like the dancer Suzanne sees.

3   Early Morning, One Brother's Birthday

For years I saw my archetype as the sister
in *The Wild Swans*, weaving cloaks to save her brothers,
captive to the evil spell. Words instead of nettles.

In turn the brothers cast their own spells: flurries
of stories of their whacked out adventures, their
puffery magic: *Now you see me, now you don't.*

Brothers gone, I'm out of a job.
Maybe it's their turn to weave a cloak
to ease my suffering? Look at them now—

how devotedly they attend to their duties!
See how their fingers bleed, weaving the nettles?
See how they hunch over, eschewing food and drink?

No, that story's a lie. The Irish in me talking.
They've got their work to do. Sweet souls,
with their own demons. Not unlike mine.

For an archetype, I turn again to the mirror:
our lanky body, *our* football shoulders, *our*
feet turned out in a duck walk...

A body, in the woods, a tall figure walking.
From a distance, could be male or female.
Now striding, now slipping, between the trees.

It's an archetype without a fairy tale, just the spirals
of DNA. Shaping. Reshaping. It's time.
Time for me to learn to walk again.

4   Diversity Includes Plankton

Suzanne positions me, again,
in front of the mirror like one of those
ancient mother gods,
arms straight out, elbows bent up at right angles,
feet planted like a tree.
I would say *willow* but the shape
is more like a *cypress*.
Dancer's body, she says.
Heron.
Giraffe, yes, also, with the spots in the light, like a popple.
Daughter dancing.
Selkie.
First mother god.
I already said that.
Brothers.
Here by the grace of god I.
Occupied with all the creatures who come through me today.
Not to forget the androgynous fish,
swimming towards the plankton and the light.
Not to forget the child,
catching the sun with her mirror.
Signaling her allies, first companions.

5   The Bird's Nest

What we call our home. Linden trees.
Silver maples. Above the river. Bird's nest.
My husband, even taller than my brothers,
wraps me in the cloak of kindness.
Luxurious feathers of reliability.
For the first time in years, I've lost weight,
even though he feeds me biscotti
with our espresso. Starry clovey taste.
I strengthen my core, content to stay
home most evenings. After supper, we curl
together on the couch. He dozes off, says,
You give good lap. Something good
is hatching. I throw an egg in the solstice
fire, ask for nourishment in the coming
year. The solstice sun on the ice
mirrors time skipping back to us: fractals,
linden blossoms, blue-black raven's feathers,
small feet on the grass.

First Blank Christmas

Some girls were singing carols

at the shiny black piano. *Hark! Hark!*

I'd dreamed that the navy smoking jacket

I'd given my brother didn't fit. It did.

He came back in that jacket and

some people got mad. *Why*

did you put us through this?

I hooked my arm in his

the way the intervention therapist

told me to do. *You're the touchy-feely one.*

A long-time friend whispered, *I keep*

thinking Lloyd's going to walk in.

He should be here, any minute now.

I told him my dream. His voice shaky.

Some girls singing. From far away.

WINTER SOLSTICE

horizon: graywater/graysky

car: crunching packed snow, heading north

coats: puffy plum puddings

you: saying poems by heart, *the mystery does not get clearer*

window: cold piney air

you: lifting from white paper smoked lake salmon

coffee: old steel thermos

twilight: constellations the color of lobelia spread across the dash

clock: stopped

solace: one round gray stone in the palm of my hand

Touchy about His Feet

My brother was touchy about his feet, known for his early run-in with a clam who latched on and wouldn't let go. He yelled, *Get it off me*, and the end of the story is when he quits yelling. My layers of memory don't know if the clam let go or he hopped to shore for someone else to loosen the bivalve bite. What I do know is: he was touchy about his feet, all of us touchy about something.

Another memory layer floats by: *something resembling happiness* when he opened my gift of socks one year—red and gray two-tone soft *soft* merino wool. Wick-Dry. He took off his boots and tried them on then and there. I took a picture of him doing that. Maybe he had his own shift back to those sepia days of the Kodak Santa who brought itchy wool slipper socks with leather bottoms and we'd get spanked and sent to our rooms before lunch and my brother would mumble as we ran up the attic steps, *Some present.*

Today another snow storm is rolling in with memories of old holidays, gifts, cold. I mark my place in the book I'm reading, *Into the Wild*. A book full of snow. Too full. Touchy, I get up and look out the window. Again, cars are going backwards on the steep hill across the street, sliding at odd angles. Again, I can't help shivering, seeing snow fall on his bones. I turn to sort the laundry Jim just brought in. I spread all my wool socks on the drying rack: some gray as the stones under riverwater, some green as the pine trees, some six shades of blue—streaks of the night sky, just before the stars.

In My Poems Since You Left Us

I worry over the menu in the Thanksgiving poem, mashed
potatoes with buttermilk and olive oil
made the night before. A harvest

poem finds roast chicken with acorn squash
which goes with brown rice, raisins
and walnuts. It's March.

In the starry Orion poem I bring to your friend,
red beets and ginger give winter strength.
Your friend says they missed you

at their potluck last weekend, though you never
used to eat anything. We split an omelette,
rich with cheese and tomatoes.

You could set a place for him anyway, I say.
Potlucks could be a holiday in motion:
your Days of Sugar Skulls. Still, I

see you, alive, sitting at the wrought iron table
outside the Birchwood, where I feasted
on cantaloupe and corn croquettes,

where you, with your *Not hungry* coffee, smoked
on the no-smoking patio, the wild
flowers gold and purple

blazing behind you. How I keep trying to feed you,
you who can no longer
say *No*.

Walking the Ice Age Trail the First Spring After

I walked from the same cabin, a different route each day. Still not too steady on my feet, I took pleasure being out in the countryside again—pines, farms, woods. The contrast of dark green and snowy hills still in March. I had to get past the pole barn to feel some wilderness. Even so, a bench showed up for a resting spot. I rested. I looked down into the wild gully. Pretend camping, for sure. When we went into town for supper, I found it amusing that people in the diner took my LEKI stick as proof of long-distance worthiness. *How many miles do you do in a day?* Sometimes I'd tell, sometimes not.

One day, I came up over a ridge, saw fluff rising up higher—goldwhite like milkweed riffling above the snow. Was it for curiosity or a winter bouquet that I walked over to it, looked down. Stopped cold when the fluff led me down to hair smoothing over a bare forehead, naked jaw, big teeth that had lost their gums. Slowly I pulled myself up from this zoomed-in focus: shifted my gaze to the whole hollow. Saw no legs, no skin, no claws. Saw a backbone long as a 20-pound Northern Pike curled into itself. Saw a few knuckles of bone, bleached out to the color of snow. *The milkweed fluff should be called hair or fur.* I took the animal for a coyote, this animal, because he had such a long jaw. I hadn't imagined before that he could've held on all winter, through the ice and snow, to his shiny hair.

A year later, I went back again. He was still there.

April, Baby

I Springfield, Missouri, the Ozarks, 1950

Daffodils and jonquils and crocus showed up for Easter
and we, awkward, posed for photos
in new church clothes. Sun grins, both of us.

Purple and golden iris bloomed on the south side of the house
where you liked to sit, cross-legged, petting Brownie the First.
Nobody could see you in that garden.

I, myself, preferred putting food coloring in glasses
to see if the creamy jonquils would turn
to scarlet, cobalt, crayon yellow.

I can see those iris leaves so clearly even today.
The place I hid the cap gun I stole from Stanley.
As if you and I were twins: *Flight* and *Fight*.

II Western Minnesota 2007

Winter Storm Watch on the prairie.
The wind drives icy specks of snow against my face.

Willows along the creek have already opened their cat paws.
A new black calf shadows her mother along the fence line.

No daffodils in sight, I pick a willow branch
to take home to the vase that holds the lupine pods,

larger than willows but just as soft, *wolf willows* I call them.
From the summer you wandered off, two years ago.

On the way back, I notice my footprints in deepening snow,
not straight and parallel like a runner's.

No. The my path looks as if alien ducks have descended,
waddled, webbed feet splayed.

I'm the only one here, so these footprints must be mine.
Or did you return to surprise me?

III   Wales 2001

Daffodils there open early March to the light winds of
the Gulf Stream, greening soft days.

Did our own lost ancestors
bring these flowers along

to their new worlds, along with their other passions—
exuberant stories and travel and drink?

Or did they simply settle down in lands that looked
familiar, New Zealand, Ozark mountains?

I like to think they brought you and me
our love of wind and stars.

IV   South Minneapolis 2005

At your memorial service, purple lupine
and dark green pine branches sprayed
out of your yellow kayak, which took the place of

a casket. The smell brought the wilderness inside.
It was July, anyway, far too late for daffodils.
Almost too late for spring lupine. No matter.

Maybe I'm the only one who remembered you
in the childhood garden, south side of the house.
Maybe I'm imagining things, anyway, like my

picture of you in a golden jacket standing backlit
at the windows of Orr Books, listening to me read
one late Sunday afternoon in winter light.

That was the only time you showed yourself for poetry,
your image a locket over my heart.
Others who loved you carry different lockets: *a song,*

a stone, a half-smile at the door... Yet all agree the lupine
spraying out of the kayak—and the wavy blue silk under it—
made a spectacular tribute, a still life

to hold you to us, to send you off, God speed.

V   Nebraska Migrations 2003

You drove to Nebraska with your old friend
to welcome the whoosh and racket
of the Sand Hill Cranes.

When you described them to me later
Your voice took on a certain exhilaration:
The rush of their wings

comes at you like a tornado, and then
you look up at the thousands of them—
it's un-fucking-believable.

I regret now I couldn't go with you.
I had to keep a distance from your van,
smoked up with your cigarettes.

Last Easter, I finally saw some,
Sand Hill Cranes, I mean, in Wisconsin,
walking along the Ice Age Trail.

They were awkward, big, and creaky—
like those driftwood sculptures
that once paraded along San Francisco Bay.

They brought back your story:

how you experienced the grace of flight.

VI   Antigua, Guatemala, Lent 2006

I followed a parade, plastic iris and daffodils
blooming at the tomb of Our Señor of the Sepulcher.

Mary lifted her arms and hands up towards *the empty tomb,*
appropriately mournful in Her Solitude.

I'm sick and tired of people asking,
Where is his body?

I swear: Mary was smiling at the flowers.
Didn't care if they were plastic or real.

So many paths to sorrow.

VII   Minneapolis Birthday 2007

You would've been 60 today, the day
I always thought was Flag Day. Purple
preferable to the red, white, and blue.

I would like to have had flown in,
from the Ozarks,
some daffodils and iris.

Or a new puppy. Brownie the Third.

VIII   Jerusalem 2007

How strange that the story of your death
matches the story of the missing body

of Jesus, you who cursed church forever
as soon as you escaped

the beatings in His Holy Name.

IX   Minneapolis Solitude 2007

Today I do what is mine to do: spring cleaning.
Wash the daffodil tea cup from Wales
and the one with hawthorn blossoms.

Ten years ago in Wales, I slept in a stone house
next to a cloud of flowering hawthorn.
My dreams unrolled a creamy scroll, a family tree

of five generations: our ancestors were lupine
and other flowers I couldn't quite make out, standing in
for all the ancestors who refused to speak of their past.

A new family tree, as in: *beautiful in mountains.*
Adaptable to flowering anywhere in the world.
More appealing than our taciturn, ribald gene pool.

Everybody loves lupine, just as everyone
loved you. Except for the times
when your refusal to talk drove us crazy.

XI   After April, Pine Lake 2006

Search and Rescue is going out again
to look for your body, their second anniversary trek.

Your disembodied voice: *I was asleep a long time*
but I'm awake now. I see a picture

of you sleeping, even though I'm the one who sleeps.
You're settled and curled in the duff, under pines,

your head resting on your right arm, your face
relaxed, your hair mingling with spring shoots of

violets, fiddlehead ferns, trillium, anemones,
not unlike those flowers in our childhood gardens.

Now you're walking towards me,
wearing the same gold you wore at Orr Books.

Even though I've said, for two years now, *I don't need his body*
to do my mourning, I'm suddenly desperate

to touch your arms, muscled and tan as you were
at twenty, ready to set off for Jackson Hole.

I want to rub them with both my hands, up and down
as though I were starting a fire.

You recede as I reach to touch you

FATHER

Laid out on the sidewalk, in a shiny navy suit,
hands folded on his belly—neither dead nor alive.

I pick up a stick thick as a baseball bat,
big enough to whack

an apology out of him. *Get up!*
I'm taking you to court for child abuse.

Whack. Whack. Whack.
Clouds of dust billow out of him

like that sudden amorphous rising
when you beat an old rug on the clothes line.

Remember that Fourth of July you
kicked the dog 27 times at the barbecue

at Minnehaha Falls? What about the time
you took my brother apart in the back yard?

Well, take this, jerk. I take out my gramma's
old farm gun, unload it into his heart. No blood

spurts out of the holes, only fumes.
Then that gray residue of fireworks oozes

itself forth. Snakes along the sidewalk.
I walk over to him and bend down close.

Lift his face by the chin. *Look at me
when I'm talking to you.* His face crumbles,

a puffball disintegrating.
The wind comes up, flings

the fruitful bodies across green fields.
There's nothing left in my hands.

A Small Change in the Map: On the Trail to Whisky Jack Lake

He stood on the trail from Angleworm to Whisky Jack Lake, all the other trails and lakes behind him. After a week of rain, it was itchy hot. He took off his raincoat, folded it, placed it under a big rock at the turn-off. In this rugged territory, there weren't any trail signs, so he didn't know that they'd changed the name of the lake to *Hungry Jack Lake*. Long before **Hungry Jack** was a brand-name. Hungry Jack, sure. He hadn't brought any food, no provisions of any kind on this day hike. But now the smell of pine smoke and frying butter in the woods sparked his interest, even his taste buds. Nothing much had interested him lately. He'd lost his job, had all the time in the world. So he kept walking down the lake trail towards the smell that soon changed from butter to bacon. A few steps more and he could swear there was fresh coffee, too. The path widened out onto a rocky shoreline beach.

A few steps across a boulder field into a clearing, following the smell, he discovered Uncle Jack himself kneeling over a camp-fire, deftly turning a pancake in an old camp skillet. Seeing Jack at the fire and the stack beside him reminded him of the child-hood word: *Flapjacks.* That brought a half smile to his face. Jack looked grand in his brand new woodsman clothes, denim and tan chamois shirt, even with the scars showing on the side of his head. It was odd, though, not to see him in his golf clothes: pressed white shorts, Kelly green knit shirt. *Here you are, son,*

Jack said. *We've been expecting you.* Jack waved him to sit down on the log that served as the sofa. A shuffle of uncles moved in from the shade, nodded *Welcome*, and milled around the circle of fire with their camp tasks. The uncle with the Coke-bottle glasses carried a full pail of wild blueberries; he picked his way over to the fire so Jack could add them to the batter. Another uncle lifted the coffeepot that was speckled like a bird's egg, *Want a cup, buddy? Free trade. Shade grown. Guatemalan.* Of course he wanted a cup, even though the uncle's hand shook so bad it spilled a trail down his arm. Another one tending the bacon, said, *When you and your sister were kids, she'd always say **more bake, more bake**, and you'd nod **yes** but wouldn't say a word. Cute as a bug's ear, you were.*

Jack's new jeans were shiny cobalt in the Coleman camp light. Before this, he'd never been camping a day in his life. Great Uncle David came walking up from the lake, looking not a day over 15, even though his body moved more like a marionette's than a person's. He lifted up a string of bass that shone in sundown light like new Sakakawea silver dollars. *What a fisherman!* howled Jack. *Those beauties will have to wait for dessert, David, or breakfast. We don't have a pan until we eat all this.* Another uncle, the one with the sweet soul and brown eyes many a woman may've fallen into was rummaging through a Duluth pack—he pulled out a golden plastic bottle shaped like a bear. *Honey!* He started juggling the bear and his Pepsi can, plus an empty bottle of blackberry brandy he'd found hidden in a hollow. He had some talent for juggling, this uncle, something never before displayed. *Give me your BlackBerries, they're no use to you here,* he crowed. All the men laughed with pleasure; the circling Ravens added their opinion. Uncle Jack called out to the gray jay, *Pipe down now, Wee-saw-kay-chak, you'll get your flapjack crusts, some bacon as well—don't get too close to the fire or we'll have to eat you too.*

Then the men started in on their family circus stories: Grandpa's circus pony, Trixie, lunging for the pond whenever anyone tried to ride her, Aunt Helen running away with the snake charmer when she was only 14, Philip talking about running away to the circus when he was 15. Did he or didn't he? When the flapjack stack was so high it was about to topple, the men drew up stumps for chairs.

Uncle Jack said, *Sit down, son. Let me serve you first. We can talk in the morning. Here at Hungry Jack Lake, all the men get to be hungry, all the men get to be fed.*

PART TWO: ECHOLOCATION: THREE DEGREES OF GRIEF

and often I dreamed you next to me,

but even then, you were always turning
down the thick corridor of trees
—Marie Howe

Narratives of loss tend often to be very
coherent; they resolve into grief.
We imagine people who have lost someone
to have grieved and to have gone on.
Nobody deals with the deepest existential
response, which is bafflement.
—Vijay Seshadri

21st Century Communion

In produce, a woman whizzes by my cart
and I see it's Christine, my fast-talking friend.
When I call out she says, *I came here to get*
cocoapowderformyMexicanchili—but I'm so

scattered today I keep finding other things—
and I want to tell you something but I can't
remember what. She winds down, then, and
I keep my news short. *I'm here for haggis.*

Cabbage. Potatoes. It's the chill in the air
that brings out the Scot in me. Her grimace,
at the mention of haggis, an invert of my smile.
It's only local lamb and oatmeal, I say. *Plus*

we'll read a funny part of 44 Scotland Street.
I gesture: *Spices that way.* She holds her list
high in her hand, prepared for this cuspy season
in a Carhartt jacket over a green Hawaiian shirt.

Then turns back. *I remember what I wanted to*
tell you. Today's the 15th Anniversary. My brother.
We stop in stopped time. It could've happened
yesterday. Tears for all our brothers. Her

15 years, my 5 and 39. My hand on her shoulder.
A long embrace in honor of not forgetting. Then
time moves. We move with it: *Time
to cook good food for the living.*

Three Friends at True Thai, Discussing the Phrase *You'll Never Get Over It*

We order an appetizer of fried purple yams. Then we each find an entrée we crave. While we wait, I tell them I've been obsessing about *American Masters: Roberto Clemente,* the first baseball player to express gratitude to his parents in Spanish on U.S. TV. The commentator lowers his voice, when he says *Clemente lost a younger sister when he was young, never got over it. Then, he, too, died a tragic death.* I ask my friends, *What's up with this phrase, never got over it—that your life is ruined if you have to live the rest of your life with tragedy?* Audrey says, *They don't want to feel uncomfortable, that's why they say that.* The yams arrive and we eat fast before the crunchy outside cools, and I'm thinking about uncomfortable people and the lavender-indigo soft yam inside stays hot as we talk. Tom says, *Well, for me, after a death you go along and you come to a place where you're not in the acute stage of grief but then something throws you back, and you're afraid you'll start sobbing in public. People might disapprove.* Yes. Now we each enjoy our own lunch and memories which we have no intention of abandoning. For me, a stir fry of tofu, mushrooms, cashews, and green onions. Good for Clemente, who let people know that his sister stayed close. Clemente, who let people know it wasn't a tragedy to live with her death, who talked about her. Who lived life to its fullest, right up until the moment his plane fell into the ocean. *Good for my friends who will talk about sorrow—good friends who talk about anything over food.*

The Family of Frederico García Lorca Stands against Exhumation of His Remains

We'd like to leave him there
By the tree at the bend in the road, the approximate spot
(They're all in good company there)
Where Frederico García Lorca and his comrades were shot.

Behind the lone *olivo*, the approximate spot
Where the Fascists buried them, made a ditch their tomb,
After their final *paseo* to that place where they were shot:
Lorca, the bullfighters, the teacher—the gravedigger too.

The Fascists buried them in a ditch, their tomb.
It's said we don't want to stir up history. That's infamy!
They say that we're homophobes, too.
This is defamation, just plain crazy!

It's said we don't want to stir up history. That's infamy!
What we want: we don't want a spectacle.
Exhumation? It adds nothing to history.
Imagine *You Tube* with Lorca's bones and skull.

We don't want a spectacle.
Do they want a relic, the bones of a saint?
Imagine *You Tube* with Lorca's skull.
The *olivo*, the ditch, the road—a sacred place.

Do they want a relic, the bones of a saint?
In the vega, swathed in its blue shimmer:
The *olivo*, the ditch, the road—it's a sacred place.
On blue and green tiles friends painted his verses,

In the vega, swathed in its blue shimmer.
Lorca and his comrades are in good company there.
On blue and green tiles friends painted his verses.
We want to leave them there.

Missing Student Found in River

This is where he was   the bluff area
walking down St. Clair Avenue
Mississippi River Boulevard   left
a party angrily   low blood sugar?
Adults have the right to be
missing   the bluff area   many people
both his friends   and those—
police   a boat   a helicopter   a dog—
who had never met him
                              This is
where he was   walking down
St. Clair   Mississippi River Boulevard
likely exhausted   in a diabetic coma
where he was   their only son
a lack of insulin?   beeps from his
Omni Pod   holding out hope
as time went on   a balloon launch
mother believed   police moved
too slowly
                    This is where he was
low blood sugar   the river
grates that catch debris   found the
body   the river   adults missing

70

walking down St. Clair   the river
at least the family   can go ahead
deal with something   more solid
than   (balloon launch
canceled)   always wondering

walking down   *This is where*

the Mississippi River

at least the family

GRADE SCHOOL PRINCIPAL AND HIS WIFE TAKE THE VISITING POET TO THE BEST RESTAURANT IN TOWN

A few too many Black Russians under his belt
turns the conversation to his wife's first husband
still MIA in Vietnam. *Why*, he says, *Why?*
How can anyone go through this year after year?
He puts his arm around her, a small blonde
in a blue silky dress. She stares, not speaking.
After the years went by, she had to go to court
to have him declared dead. But why?
How could she go on? From her eyes, I
understand that she loves this man, both of them
haunted by the missing space of her first
husband, the many ways he may have died.
The many ways he may have lived and
not returned. Missing in infinite actions.

It's almost midnight with a long drive
home tomorrow on icy roads.
I can't think of anything to say
to his passion other than *It must be a*
tremendous loss, one with no end.
Licking the rim, where the Kahlua
and cream sidle towards his mouth
and tongue, he continues: *What is it*
all about? I mean, what's the purpose?

Confused by this tipsy lurch off topic
I ask, *War? Are you thinking about the*
wars that keep going on?

No, no. Not war, he says. *The Big Bang,*
the creation, the stars with their exploding
questions. What's it all about? Our lives?
Our love? Our suffering? I lean back
in the leatherette booth. I pause, say,
I don't know. I write the poems about my life.
I read them to people. I can't remember
the exact line in my friend's poem, but quote it
anyway. *Poets stagger along behind the crowd.*
The blue woman rubs her husband's arm.
Her rings sparkle like stars against his dark
navy suit. *Darling, let's call it a night.*

Still Missing: 500,000

—After watching Alice Walker on Book TV

Walker says 500,000 *children are missing in Iraq.*
I have no reason to doubt her. In the absence
of names, she holds a pair of child's shoes,
sacred objects, each strap a crayon color:
forest green, sky blue, fire engine red. I trail away
from the TV, wondering about the names of the
children. Lost. Kidnapped. Sold. Tortured.
Hidden. Killed. Who can say all of their names?

I know the name of one boy kidnapped
twenty years ago. Let his be the name for today.
You could sketch the scene: Use colors good
for warm October evenings, maple trees,
a country road, three boys riding bikes home
from the video store. A man steps into the road
from the woods or maybe from a car, maybe
a Chevy, like cars all over the world. The man
wears a mask, carries a gun. He orders the boys
to lie face-down in the ditch. *Who's the oldest?*
One of the boys stands up, the man takes him.
Tells the other two, *Run or I'll shoot.* Now sketch in
a car driving away, or a man leading a boy into

the darkening woods. One bike wheel spinning
in the ditch. Where is the video? You decide.
Now pick up a gray crayon, rip off the paper,
turn it on its side and scribble over all
the colors, show childhood gone awry.

Now pick up your darkest charcoal, work
its edge. Line in the cattails, the cornstalks,
the miles and miles of empty fields. Listen
for the cicadas ululating in the dark, as they do
in every country of our world. Listen to the
the families and friends: 500,000 plus one.
Their high-pitched, belly-deep, husky, and
keening cries. *Jacob. Jacob. Jacob.*
Jacob.

Heartland MIA

1

He won't come out of his apartment,
my friend's brother, where 'Nam
rages every day and night. Nightmares.
He's cut off most of the family, the ones
who did the intervention, *accusing him*
of drinking to self-destruction.

The family prays for a miracle.

2

The man lets his younger brother
pick him up for lunch one Sunday afternoon.
The brother is alarmed that the whites of his eyes
have yellowed, his legs too weak to walk.

Which brother is more fearful of the sense
of death in the air? Which one expects
a miracle?

3

The brother who is ill
opens his door to a total stranger, a friend,
a vet, a friend of Bill W. 's—a man
who's ridden out his need to drink.
The stranger works a miracle.
(What does he say to the brother? Does he

ask to *only touch the hem of your garment*?)
No matter. The brother who is ill goes with him
to the V.A., agrees to stay (if only for a day).

The family prays for a miracle.

4
Is it a miracle to be comforted
by a stranger's love? Is it enough
of a miracle if, before you die, you recognize
that another has suffered as you have?
Is it a miracle if you are touched by love
for only one day?

5
In the evenings, I walk in my neighborhood.
I, also, pray for miracles.
Pray to let go of my anger at the universe
because miracles didn't arrive on demand.
Pray that if one comes, I'll recognize it.
Such faint Scottish faith. July 5th,
I stop at the day lilies that glow stain-glass
at sundown, much better than fireworks,
along with wild roses, blue bells. The house
where the POW-MIA flag still flies—

6
Pray for the POWs still lost
in the V.A. hospital down the river road,
our war, and the soldiers from the new wars,
their wars, which are also *ours*.

Love, Salvage

—After watching a documentary on Glenn Gould

Counselors tell you, *Addiction*
is a love affair with chemicals.
An addict can't pay attention

to your conversation. He can only say,
Oh, I didn't know it was that bad/
that good. Here, call this number.

You're in that *Far Side* cartoon with the dog:
blah blah GINGER, blah blah blah GINGER.
But how can that be true, when he was

so charming, affectionate, playful, talented?
How can he walk away in his long black coat,
long scarf, leather gloves, black hat?

You wanted a conversation with him. You
wanted to ask him, gingerly, *Did you love me?*
Now, you've stopped wanting. You've opened

your arms to the love *you have for him.*

Who's Missing on Mt. Everest?

the guide Rob Hall made it to the Summit
made it up the Hillary Step—
that final crack in rock and ice to the peak—
even though it was slow going with the guide ropes
sailing out in the gale-force winds
like double dutch jump ropes going mad—
everyone waiting their turn
long past the turnaround time breathing their
precious oxygen taking baby steps in astronaut suits

the guide Rob Hall helped his client Doug up
that treacherous Hillary Step up from the treacherous
traverse (which you may not know means
walking across a ridge that isn't wide
enough for you to place two feet side by side)
it was one hour   *two hours*   past turnaround time—
what was he thinking, that guide?—
and now it was time to go down
the others were making their descent—
a hurricane of icy winds blew the ropes—
blew their faces and hands—Doug
was out of oxygen   his reserves used up

the guide called base camp on the phone
asking someone to bring up oxygen from
the South Summit (just a short hike in

good weather—in *mountaineering terms*)
imagine—they were too high to be rescued—
air so thin it can't bear the weight
of a helicopter and winds so violent no human
could skate back up that knife edge ridge of snow
so soon after coming back down—the guide had told his wife
if you can't walk down, you might as well
be on the moon—the voice the only thing
that can fly that high

2

later when the storm abated
and many people were dead or missing
when climbers could approach the summit again
they found Rob the guide curled up in
a hollow of snow—like a crescent moon—
oxygen tanks in a row and axes   yes   the axe the last thing
a climber lets go of in the snow—
would you call this Rob *missing*?
no. he is *not missing*.
his family has a picture of his shape snow-dusted
under a blue sky. they can hold on to that
and his axe   even if his life is gone   even if
his friend could not bear to take a token off his body
even if his body can never be recovered.

but what about Doug   whose body was never found?
is he *missing*?   what picture does his family
hold in their mind's eye? the axe that was found
where the ropes stop on the Cornice Traverse

a dangerous place—a little way above Rob's body?
it might be his. (an axe is the last thing a climber
lets go of). maybe they imagine him free-flying down
the 10,000 Kanshung Face or sleep-tumbling
down the Southwest Face. maybe they
imagine him being discovered 5,000 years from now
like the Man in the Alps. maybe they can make a picture
from Rob's words on the phone at 5:31 a.m. when he called
from the South Summit below the traverse—*Doug is gone.*

so would you say Doug is *missing on Everest*?
yes. he is one of the *missing ones.*   if families have no
body   no voice   no picture   they need at least a
a story to contain the body. something more than
the blurry absences of Everest   the vast white-outs
the avalanches that move and make new drop-offs every day.

Part Three: Navigation: Standing Still

When their bones are picked clean and the clean bones gone,
They shall have stars at elbow and foot...
—Dylan Thomas

I step into the day, I step into myself, I step into
mystery.
—Anishinaabe morning prayer

THE LABYRINTH, WINTER SOLSTICE

I am grateful, Solitude, for this day of croissants,
and yoghurt, for 10,000 years of women's history,
for the snow, the color of the moon. Grateful, too,

for these consonant sounds my men's shoes make
walking up the ice-on-gravel road. Grateful to
see the soft spot the labyrinth makes in snow:

A fontanel! on the bald round crown of hill.
It's waiting for the wheel to carry us to summer,
for prairie grasses to wisp like a baby's curls.

I'll come back then for a brisk sit in the sun.
Take off my shoes. Remember the days
we ran barefoot in green shadows of the corn.

Yes, I'm grateful, Solitude, for all my other lives,
even the years I lost my footing, circling round.
Grateful for this moon snow day

that turns me, my Solitude, back to you.

Have Drum Will Journey

1

Why do Swedes love their little red horses at winter solstice? Why do the Sami wear red?

2

The solstice lingers more than one day—we cheer it on from ancient fear the sun won't move again, even though we know it is the earth that is shifting on its axis. Some go inward and dream like shamans, tying up loose ends of the year. Some light fires, bang pots and pans. Light candles, wave shiny paper.

10

When Lloyd died, all the other relatives who'd made sudden exits circled my living room like the men in *Truly Madly Deeply*. *What do they want?* I asked my friends. Of course the holidays are difficult.

4

Some Celtic Americans talk of shamanism, especially when they return to customs at winter solstice. To be a shaman, you have to have a community that will help you re-enter, feed you, which few do in this day and age. What have we lost, what have we gained giving up the past?

8

Once I dreamed a mermaid dream of broken glass on granite steps of a university, my feet bled red. The dream voice said, *Your poems are not here.* Instantly I dream-traveled to my dining room with my big table, the room with the red paisley curtains.

7

One of my students from another place wrote a story about the shaman riding his sick relative back to health. I won't disclose the details. But the colors red and blue came into play. The shaman had a community to bring him back. What I recall about the story is the word **ride.** Of course, the shaman still rides, disguised as Santa.

15

In the far north there are ancient rock carvings that show a figure flying from one reindeer to another. A dotted arc marks the path. Three or four repetions of the figure on the arc turn the rock into a flipbook.

6

An old friend studied these ancient shamanic arts for over five years—one side of his card reads: *Have Drum Will Journey;* the other lists his *bona fides* as an engineer. This makes him more credible to me.

13

I'm writing not only for those who died suddenly, but also for those who mourn them. The ones who over-winter, waiting to bring flowers to the markers, the cairns, the place last-touched.

9

This solstice, again, I was surprised to discover my brother's Christmas ornament, a tiny pewter Swedish horse, the size of a thimble, tied with a grosgrain red ribbon.

16

The old Scandinavian calendar, **Primstaven,** looks like a yard stick, the year in two halves, winter on one side, summer the other. Notches and carvings tell the story of the seasons— animals, weather, saints.

11

One summer solstice, two years ago, the other side of winter, I traveled to see my journeying friend. I fell asleep sprawled under a canopy of summer green trees. When he came out of the house, he told me, *Spirit wants me to drum circles around you, for your low energy.* He said, *Don't talk. The dead ones don't need anything from you.* He walked slowly around me. Around. Around. (Should I even be writing this?) My heart pounded, the smell of trees filled my lungs, my heart came out of me like a vision and doubled, then shimmered *red red red,* in triple time.

13

Today I'm using a red brush to cross off old calendar dates. It's too cold to go out. I'll stay home, write, cook. Red weaves its way down this page.

14

The shamans across the polar circle know when to ride, when to stand still.

LEAVING THE NEW BOOK ON GRIEF

You settle your bones into a river of words.
Imagine a beautiful place and, of course,

You're walking in the woods careful of logs fallen on the trail.
So far from the illumined city.

Intricacies of leaves and ferns. *Imagine a guide,* she says.
Your brother appears a little off the earth like Orion.

Outlined in gold lights, hovering.
The lights could be gold and blue lightning bugs or gold stars.

Your brother is your other half, more than a lover or husband.
DNA turned inside out, unfolding in myriad paths.

He could no more give up his wilderness wandering
than you could give up scribbling into your dreams.

Let this guide come into your dreams tonight.
Stars enter the new book on grief, as they do in the old books.

Is your brother getting ready to leave for the sky?
Orion is the Mayan *Maize God,* the one who leaves, returns.

In your sleep, your lit-up brother comes back in another shape—
A poet-hiker friend who says, *I think I proved to them to love poetry.*

A garbled sentence but even so a message from starry wilderness.
Your brother's blessing for your risk-strewn path.

Walking the Trail to Angleworm Lake,
Six Years after He Did

Here I am at the hot sunny Angleworm Trailhead,
with a friend. I thought I'd never come here because
I still couldn't walk the whole seven miles. Last year
it occurred to me I could walk one mile in and back out.
I've filled out the BWCAW Visitor's Self-Issued Permit.
When it asks *Method of Travel*, I skip *canoe, dogsled, ski,
snowshoe, motorboat, kayak, other.* Circle as he did: *foot.*
On the line that says *Trip Leader* I sign my own name and
fill in the *Party of 2* with date. Drop the cardstock copy down
the slot of the wooden box attached to the bulletin board
that announces conditions on the trail. I've touched his
last point of human connection and that's when the tears
start to come. Are my hands on this rough wood enough?

No, the shadows of the green woods tell me I'm not done.
My friend takes a photo of me by the bulletin board.
We start out slowly, reveling in the cool air that hits us
the minute we're in the shade. I keep looking down
at the dusty trail so I won't catch my shoe on tree roots.
Which gives me a good eye for wildflowers, ferns.
My friend, slender as a wood sprite, leads the way—
she scans the hills and trees, stops to take a picture
of a spider web in a gnarly oak. I document us
with a shot of her walking ahead, hair ablaze.

Now that we're walking, I relax into the motion.
Walking has its way with me. The wind through
the tree tops sings its story of summers past. They
talk in many languages: *Si-si-gwa-d. Susurrus.*
So much rain this June, like the June he walked here.
Again, late wild flowers. The same new green growth
of the pines that he saw, not scraping our faces but
brushing them. The little yellow flowers were here then,
the ones we can't remember the name of. We do know
that the butterfly that alights on them is a swallowtail.
The bunchberry lights up the trail with their white blossoms.
The miniature false lilies of the valley—I'd rename them
fairy house trees—hide behind them. Climbing higher,
we see more white flowers like stars against the dark sky
of forest floor. *Starflowers*—surely he noticed these.

We stop for lunch and water, a downed pine our sofa.
Sit a long time in the light and shadow, looking. How
I miss the smell of this air when I'm in the city.

> Underfoot, pine needles
> At eyelevel, newgreen fans.
> Mix of past & *now.*

The yellow topographical map says we're almost
to the lake but my feet say *turn around.* The yellow
of the map brings back early trips, me in a young
woman's body in a bathing suit, in a canoe, hot,
feet touching the cool canoe bottom, skin on skin.

We turn back to present time, gather up our day-hike
supplies, start walking back to the car. My left foot
is lagging. I concentrate on the roots. *Brother,*
did you get this tired? On my right, a flash of pink
interrupts fatigue. Lady's Slipper. *Pink Moccasin.*
We bend down to stare—*spellbound* you could say—
rising ivory lily leaves above two dark-veined bright-
pink bulbs, silky fragile shells protecting empty space—
it survives on filtered light under jack pines, reindeer moss its
sweet companion. My friend murmurs, *Your brother*
sent this to you today. Grateful for the world of beauty,
and you in it.

Notes on the Poems
and Some Commentaries on Process

Part One
Section Page

The original Spanish poem by Antonio Machado, 1885-1939 reads: *Caminante, no hay camino / se hace camino al andar.*

The quote by Pauline Boss is from *Ambiguous Loss: Learning How to Live with Unresolved Grief,* Harvard University Press, 1999, Kindle Edition, location 163.

"Neither Here Nor There"
The poem the friend paraphrases is "Lost" by David Wagoner, from *Collected Poems, 1956-1976,* Indiana University Press, 1979.

The book *Lost in the Wild: Danger and Survival in the North Words,* by Cary J. Griffith, Borealis Books, 2007, delineates the Search and Rescue procedures with a close study of two different men lost in the BWCAW, one of whom was an experienced guide.

Abby is a reference to Abby Sciuto, a character on the popular TV show, *NCIS.* She is played by Pauley Perette.

"Cold Up North"
The quote is from Spencer Reece's poem, "A Bestiary, iv., The Bat," page 9 in *The Clerk's Tale,* Mariner Books, 2004.

"MY BROTHER'S TEARS"

Jefferson Barracks was built in 1826 to replace Fort Bellefontaine. It was the first military base west of the Mississippi. It was established as a national cemetery in 1866; the first person buried was an infant daughter of an officer.

"FIRST SUMMERS AND THE LAST:
THE BOY WHO SLEPT UNDER THE STARS"

I wrote this at the Summer Solstice, June 2005, in a form inspired by the Dakota Winter Count. I then read it at the memorial for my brother, July 1st, 2005. When my brother was in the wild, he liked to sleep outside his tent, on the ground, under the stars, in all seasons. I did not intend for stars to be a recurring image in this book, but apparently my brother and my dreams did.

"LLOYD LLOYD"

Winter's Bone, a 2010 film directed by Debra Granik, with the screenplay adapted from the novel by Daniel Woodrell, won the Sundance Grand Jury Prize (U.S. Drama) and the Waldo Salt Screenwriting award.

The quote *Mornings were reserved for remorse and sweet tea...* is from the memoir *A Lie about My Father* by John Burnside, Graywolf Press, 2007.

"MESSING AROUND IN BOATS"

For Gayla.

The quote is from *Wind in the Willows,* by Kenneth Graham, Methuen, London, 1908. Kindle Edition, location 77.

Gayla Ellis joined a wilderness trip on a houseboat on Lake Powell, organized by Lloyd and some friends that included climbers and their other friends who weren't as active as the climb-ers. And, as usual, my brother slept on the ground even though there was a houseboat available. Gayla remembers the group reading books out loud after supper and laughing, especially *A Walk in the Woods: Rediscovering America on the Appalachian Trail*, by Bill Bryson, Anchor; 2nd edition available 2006.

"BUT WERE YOU MAD?"

Basic wilderness rules come in some variation of the following, as brought to public attention in the film *127 Hours: Tell some-one where you're going, when you're coming out, then call when you get out. Call with any change of plans. Agree with your friend/s that if you don't call by the set time, they should call the sheriff.*

For specific information about safety guidelines of the BWCAW, (details you may or may not know), see the 2011 or a current *BWCAW Trip Planning Guide*, at any Ranger Station. You can also check out www.fs.usda.gov/superior. For example, I didn't know until Lloyd went missing that the Forest Service doesn't have a consistent method for checking the day hikers' *Visitor's Self-Issued Permits*. The BWCAW covers too many miles of road to collect permits every day. I wrote this poem in 2011 looking back at my stew of angers (in 2005), a common part of grief.

"AUTUMNAL"

The quote is from *Into the Wild* by Jon Krakauer, Random House, 1997; Large Print Edition, Anchor, 2009, page 205.

"WHAT IT WAS LIKE TODAY"

This braided prose poem was inspired by the work of Deborah Keenan and Jim Moore, whose poems with this title tend to be shorter and tighter, focused on events of one day.

This one-day's truth worked for me here, although I used the concept in a different form.

"My Assigned Humans and Myself"
The phrase *assigned humans* is from the poem "Hope" in the collection *Good Heart*, by Deborah Keenan, Milkweed Editions, 2003.

"Mirror: Solstice Sun"
The image of figures walking between the trees is an image-echo from Flannery O'Connor's introduction to her novel *Wise Blood*, Harcourt, Brace & Company, 1952.

"Winter Solstice"
For Jim.
After May Swenson.

"Touchy About His Feet"
The phrase *something resembling happiness* is another quote from *Into the Wild*, page 224.

"A Small Change in the Map:
On the Trail to Whisky Jack Lake"
Wee-saw-kay-chak is the Ojibwe word referring to a *Gray Jay* or *Canadian Jay*, also known as Camp Robber. *Jejak* means a larger bird. *Wisa ke* means "singed" or "burnt"; therefore, the "hangs around by the fire" definition makes a lot of sense. English speakers turned the word into *Whisky Jack*.
Thanks to Heid and Lise Erdrich for help with the Ojibwe.

My brother's clothing was found on the trail to Whisky Jack Lake, the last physical sign of his earthly life.

PART TWO
Section Page

The Marie Howe quote is from "Gretel, from a sudden clearing" in *The Good Thief*, Persea Books, 1988.

In a friend's book, I found an (undated) interview with Vijay Seshadri from *Poets & Writers;* this particular part refers to his poem "Disappearances," from *The Long Meadow*, Graywolf, 2004.

"21ST CENTURY COMMUNION"
For Michael Sikorski, Christine's brother, and for my brothers, Lloyd and Philip Skelton.

"THREE FRIENDS AT TRUE THAI, DISCUSSING
THE PHRASE *YOU'LL NEVER GET OVER IT*"
The poem refers to the narrator of *American Masters: Roberto Clemente*, PBS.

"THE FAMILY OF FREDERICO GARCÍA LORCA STANDS
AGAINST EXHUMATION OF HIS REMAINS"
This is a found pantoum from *The New Yorker*, June 22, 2009, page 48. The phrases in italics are either Spanish words untranslated in the article, or translated quotes from Lorca.

"MISSING STUDENT FOUND IN RIVER"
In memory: Dan Zamlen.
This is a found poem from *The StarTribune* A1, A11, May 2, 2009.

"STILL MISSING: 500,000"

In memory: Jacob Wetterling, still missing, and the missing children of Iraq, perhaps 2,000,000 since Walker's broadcast.

Accounts of Jacob Wetterling's disappearance have varied somewhat over the twenty plus years he's been missing; this poem may or may not be the up-to-date version in the police files.

"LOVE, SALVAGE"

The last stanza is a paraphrase of one of Gould's stepchildren, who stated his desire to talk with Gould later in life—but Gould died too soon. The PBS documentary *American Masters: Genius Within: The Inner Life of Glenn Gould* aired December 27, 2010. Cartoonist Gary Larson created the cartoon about Ginger, one of his *Far Side* drawings.

"WHO IS MISSING ON EVEREST? "

I've worked on many versions of poems about the drive to conquer Everest (the word *conquer* used cautiously), specifically poems that deal with the disastrous May 10-11, 1996 storms during which eight people died. Resources include *Storm Over Everest* on *FRONTLINE,* a film by David Breashears, *Into Thin Air* by Jon Krakauer, and conversations with Lloyd about this tragedy and *The Perfect Storm.*

This poem is for Rob Hall and Doug Hanson and their families. And for all the sherpas who have died helping Westerners climb Chomolungma, Goddess Mother of Mountains, *also called* Sagarmatha.

"AND DEATH SHALL HAVE NO DOMINION"

On the Poetry Foundation website we read: Ralph Maud, in *Entrances to Dylan Thomas's Poetry,* declared that the writer's first published poem was the subsequently popular "And death shall have no dominion," which appeared on May 8, 1933, in the *New English Weekly.* http://www.poetryfoundation.org/bio/dylan-thomas, accessed March 11, 2011.

The Anishinaabe prayer is quoted by Pauline Boss in *Ambiguous Loss.*

"THE LABYRINTH IN WINTER"

With gratitude for Clare's Well, *Spirituality Farm,* in Annandale, Minnesota, where I wrote some of these poems.

"HAVE DRUM WILL JOURNEY"

After Kimoko Hahn.
The numbers indicate the chronology of each section's composition, over two years.

The Latin for solstice is *sol stetit.* Mid-13c. from O. Fr. *solstice,* from L. *solstitium,* point *at which the sun seems to stand still,* from *sun* (see *sol*) + pp. stem of *sistere, to come to a stop, make stand still.* In this way solstice embodies the wait for change, even if the wait is anxiety-tinged.

Truly, Madly, Deeply is a 1990 U.S. film about grief and its complications. The main character is totally heartbroken at the death of her boyfriend, but is even more unprepared for his return as a ghost, with his ghostly friends.

"Walking the Trail to Angleworm Lake, Six Years after He Did"

The haiku in this poem came to me when I stepped out of the car in the North Woods of Minnesota—in response to the smell of woods and water and air. In that way, the whole poem is a kind of haibun for the haiku, if not in the traditional arrangement.

Si-si-gwa-d is the Ojibwe word for sounds the trees make, as reported in the Glossary in *Night Flying Woman: An Ojibway Narrative*, by Ignatia Broker, Minnesota Historical Society Press, 1983, p. 135.

As I completed the manuscript, and wrote this last poem, I thought of others who've lost a sibling and the thought came to me, *May you find as many acts of ritual as you need.* Then a quote returned to me, from one of the first books I read about grief: *There is no other loss in adult life that appears to be so neglected as the death of a brother or sister.* It's from *How to Go on Living When Someone You Love Dies*, Therese A. Rando, Bantam, 1991, page 153.

Notes on the Boundary Waters, now named the BWCAW, The Boundary Waters Canoe Area Wilderness:

Some people say it is one of the four most beautiful places in the world. One thing is sure: It casts a spell on people and draws them back time and time again. The Ojibwe (some prefer the name Anishinaabe) lived there and further south for a long time before Europeans arrived to explore, convert, and engage in fur trading. The Ojibwe are one of the largest groups of indigenous people living in the U.S. and Canada.

The BWCAW, on the border of Northern Minnesota and Canada, has changed little since the glaciers melted. With more than 1,000 lakes and streams, 1,500 miles of canoe routes, and nearly 2,200 designated campsites, the BWCAW draws over 250,000 visitors each year. It was recognized as a prime location for recreational opportunities in 1926. But it wasn't until October 21, 1978, that The Boundary Waters Canoe Area Wilderness Act was established to provide specific guidance for managing the million plus acres.

A new mining project currently threatens the water quality of the lakes where wild rice, the sacred food of the Ojibwe, grows, as well as the water quality of the entire wilderness. When I first canoed the Boundary Waters, in 1963, I could drink the water right out of the lakes. Think of how many lifetimes of pure water have been there since the glaciers passed down this way. Will the water be pure for all the lifetimes to come?

Words of Gratitude from the Author

I SEND OUT HUGE HUGS OF GRATITUDE TO FRIENDS AND FAMILY who read or listened to some of these poems before they turned into a manuscript and now a book. Your friendships kept me going when I had no idea where I or the random poems were going. I'm grateful also to those who offered *shelter in the storm* out of the city: Joan Drury who sustained Norcroft for many years; Pat and Ed Pendleton; Audrey Anderson; Sheila and Don Thomsen; Clare's Well and friends who did the driving. Gratitude also for Theresa Plummer's quiet listening when I repeated the same stories over and over; for my spiritual community at Lyndale UCC; for my husband Jim Smith who has listened to many drafts of the poems, with his patience and attention, saying, *That sounds like you.*

Thanks to those writers who read and commented on the poems and/or the manuscript at various stages: Five Daughters Writing Group, Diane Frank and her Blue Light Poetry Class, Margaret Hasse, Barbara L. Jones, Deborah Keenan, Shannon King, Jim Moore, and Cary Waterman. To Joe and Nancy Paddock who read the whole manuscript out loud, thank you for your kind and thoughtful gift.

A heart-felt thank you to Jim Perlman, publisher of Holy Cow! Press for his belief in my work and his continuing support of poetry, books, and community. Thanks to all the others who took part in the publishing process, especially: The Minnesota

State Arts Board, who funded a grant for manuscript preparation and travel; Christine Sikorski, who proof-read and edited the manuscript; artist Karen Morrill, whose painting graces the cover; Beth Gedatus, who coaxed relaxation out of me for a photograph. Lastly, appreciative thanks to the writers who took time away from their own work to read the manuscript and write a cover comment.

Thanks to the named and unnamed writers, students, friends, and readers, who keep the love and practice of poetry alive.

ABOUT THE AUTHOR

THE BOY WHO SLEPT UNDER THE STARS IS ROSEANN LLOYD'S
fourth collection of poetry. She's previously published eight
books, including three collections of her poetry, *Because of the
Light* (Holy Cow! Press, 2003), *War Baby Express* (Holy Cow!
Press, 1996, awarded the Minnesota Book Award for Poetry,
1997), and *Tap Dancing for Big Mom,* (New Rivers Press, 1986).
Her other books include: two nonfiction books for Harper/
Hazelden; the translation of a novel from Norwegian, for Seal
Press; the anthology she co-edited with Deborah Keenan,
Looking for Home: Women Writing About Exile, (Milkweed
Editions, 1990), which received an American Book Award in
1991. *The Boy Who Slept Under The Stars* is also available in an
electronic eBook format.

Her other awards include an Artist Fellowship from the Bush
Foundation, a Fellowship at the Civitella Ranieri Artists
Center, in Umbertide, Italy, and several Loft McKnight grants.
Her new book was completed with a grant from the Minnesota
State Arts Board. In 2008 *City Pages* named her *Artist of the
Year* (in poetry). Her work has appeared in many literary jour-
nals and anthologies, as well as on *The Writer's Almanac*.

Roseann Lloyd lives in Minneapolis and makes a living teach-
ing at the Loft and working as an adjunct professor at sev-
eral colleges and universities in the Twin Cities. She also does
manuscript consulting; she's available for public talks and
readings. Please visit her website, www.roseannlloyd.com.